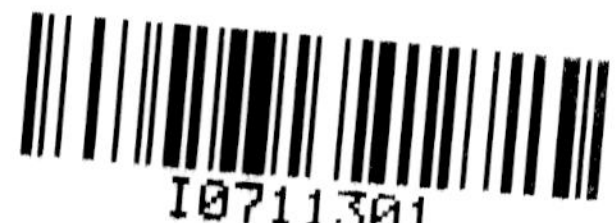

THIS COLORING BOOK BELONG TO

....

....

....

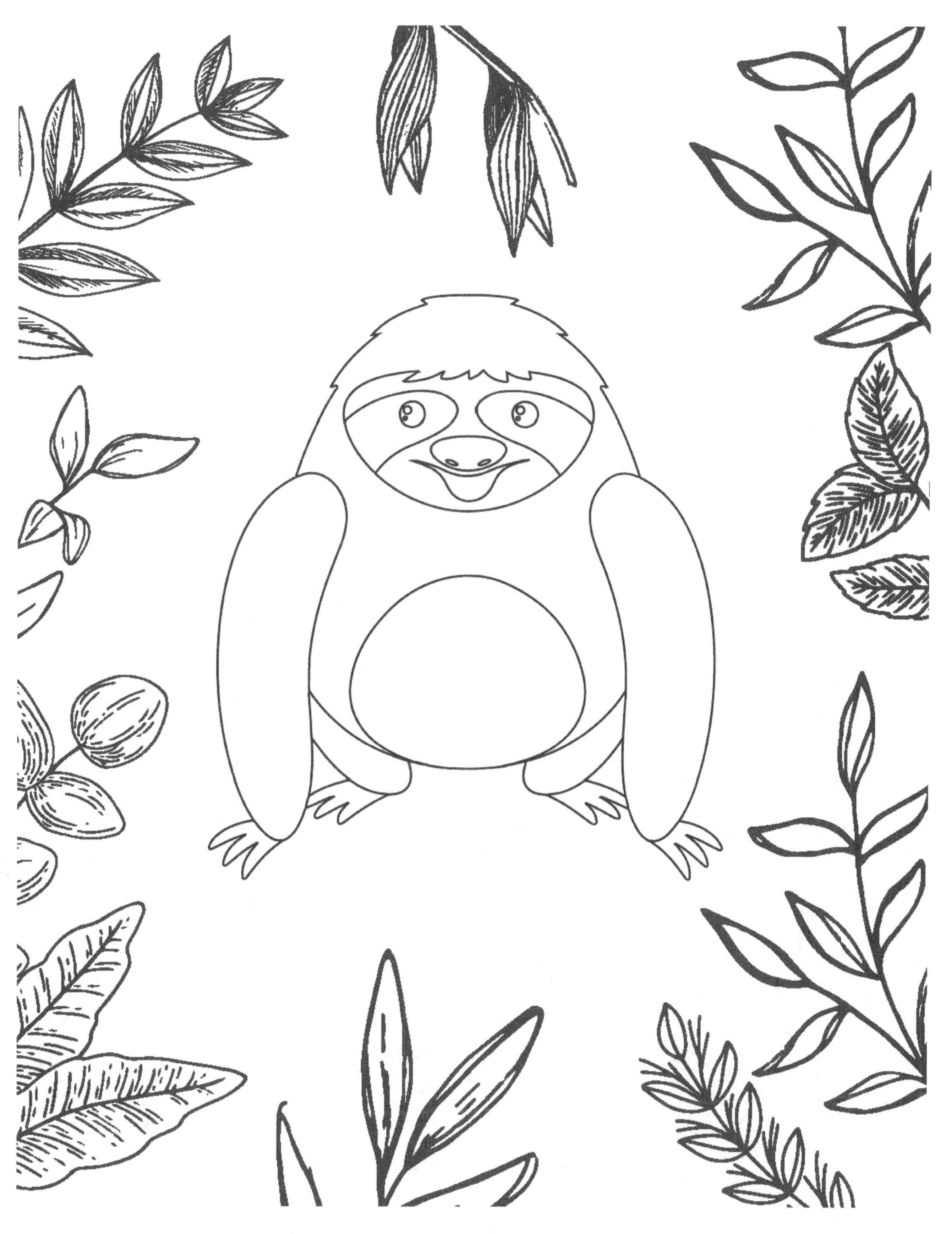

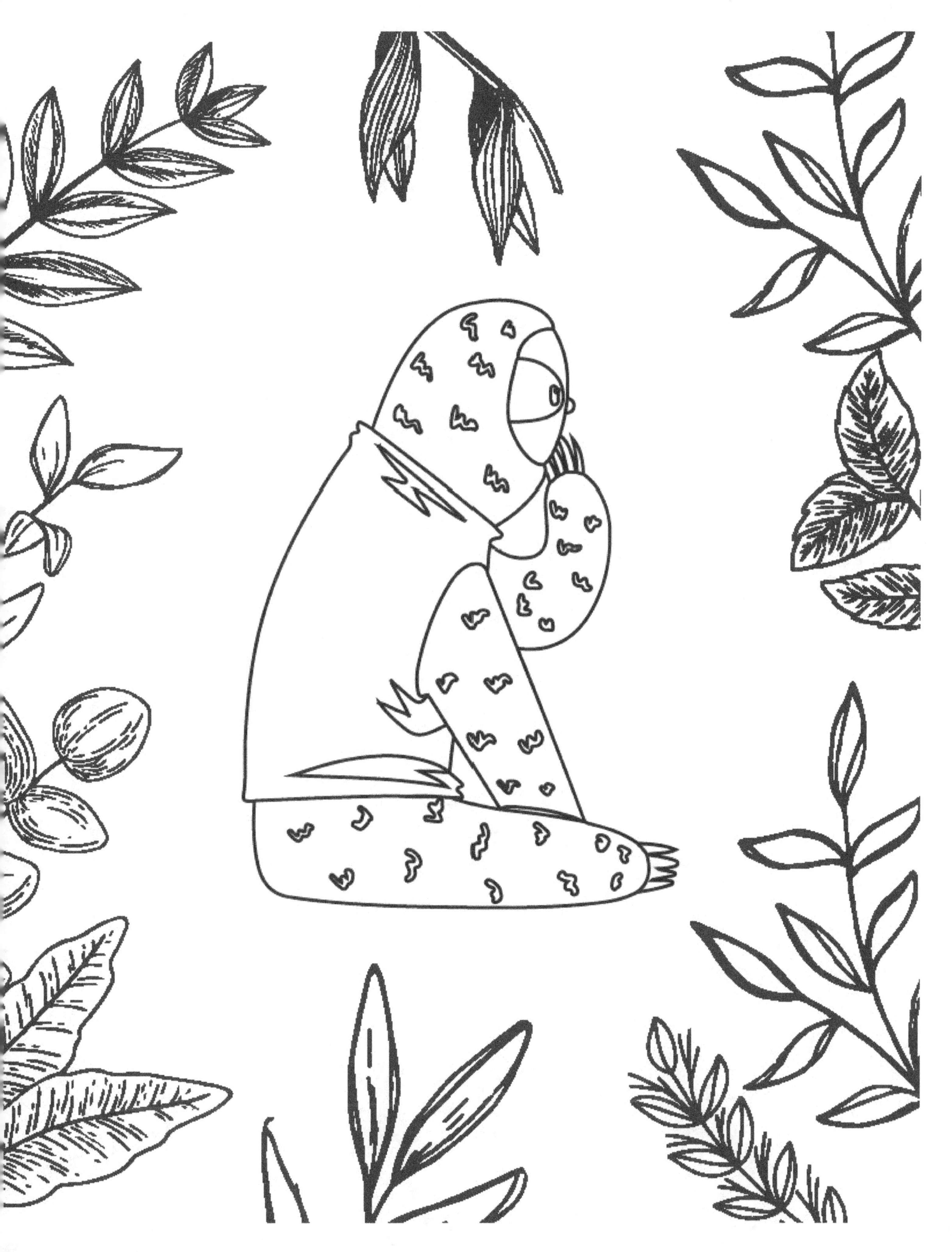

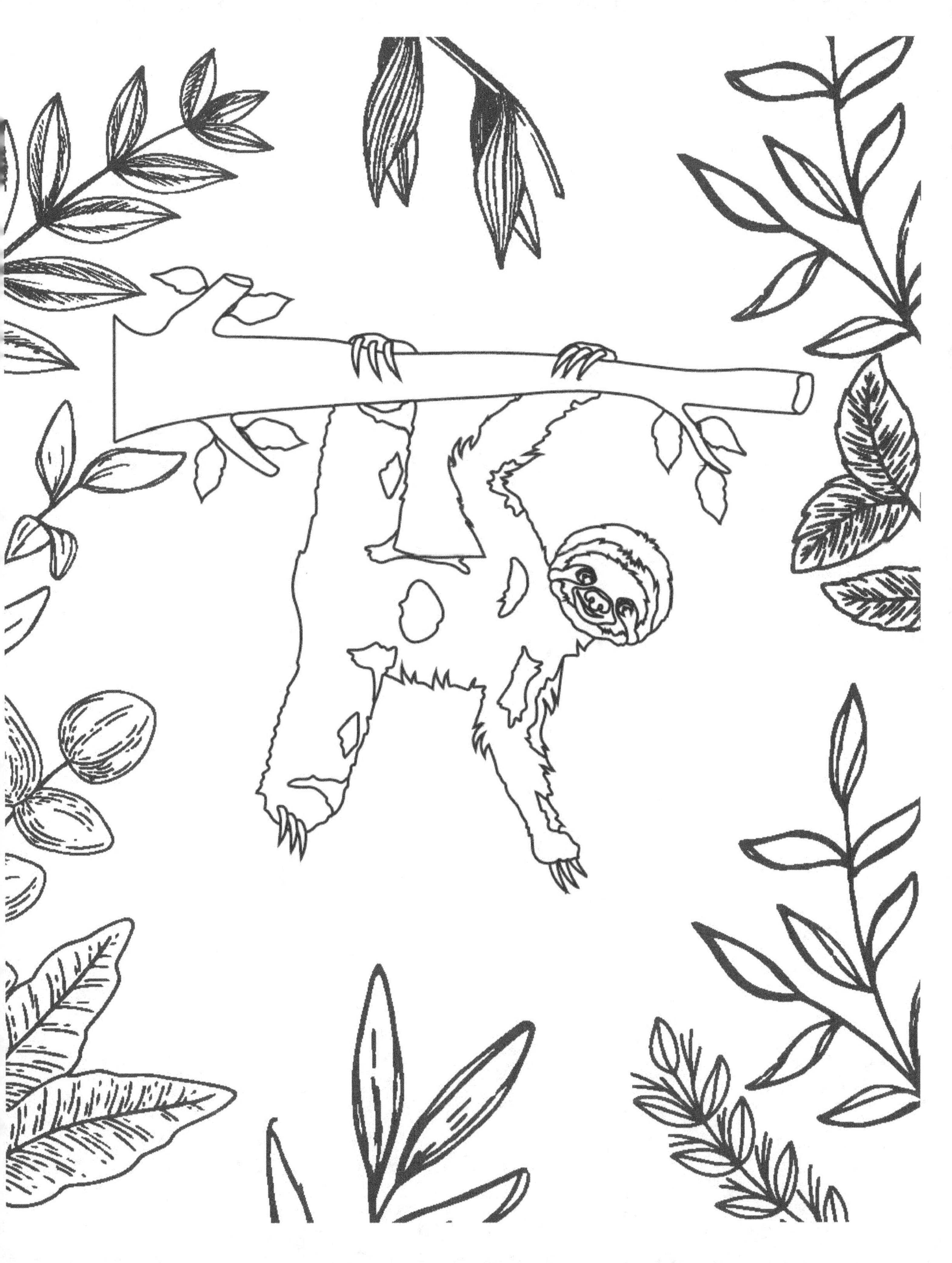

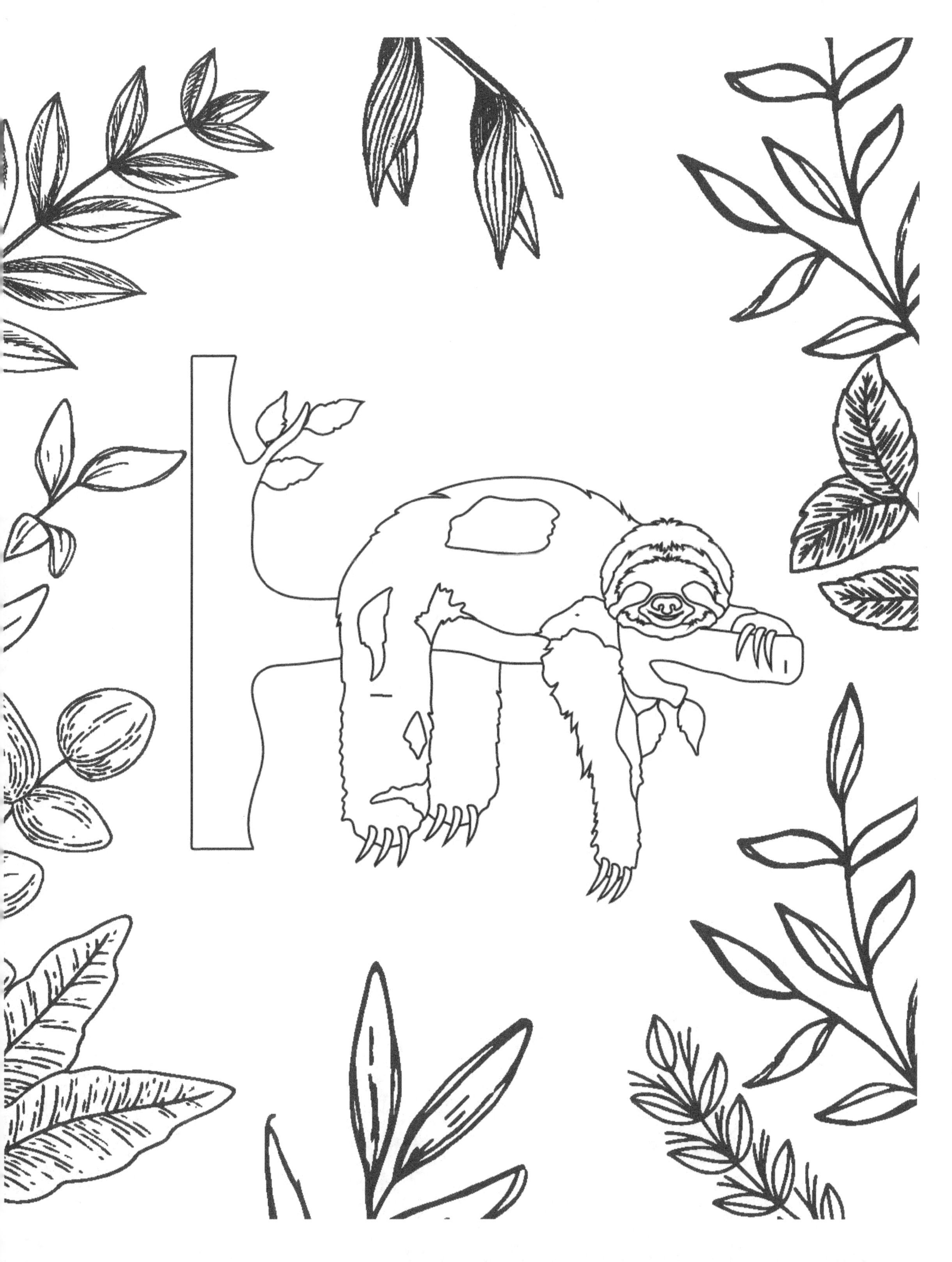

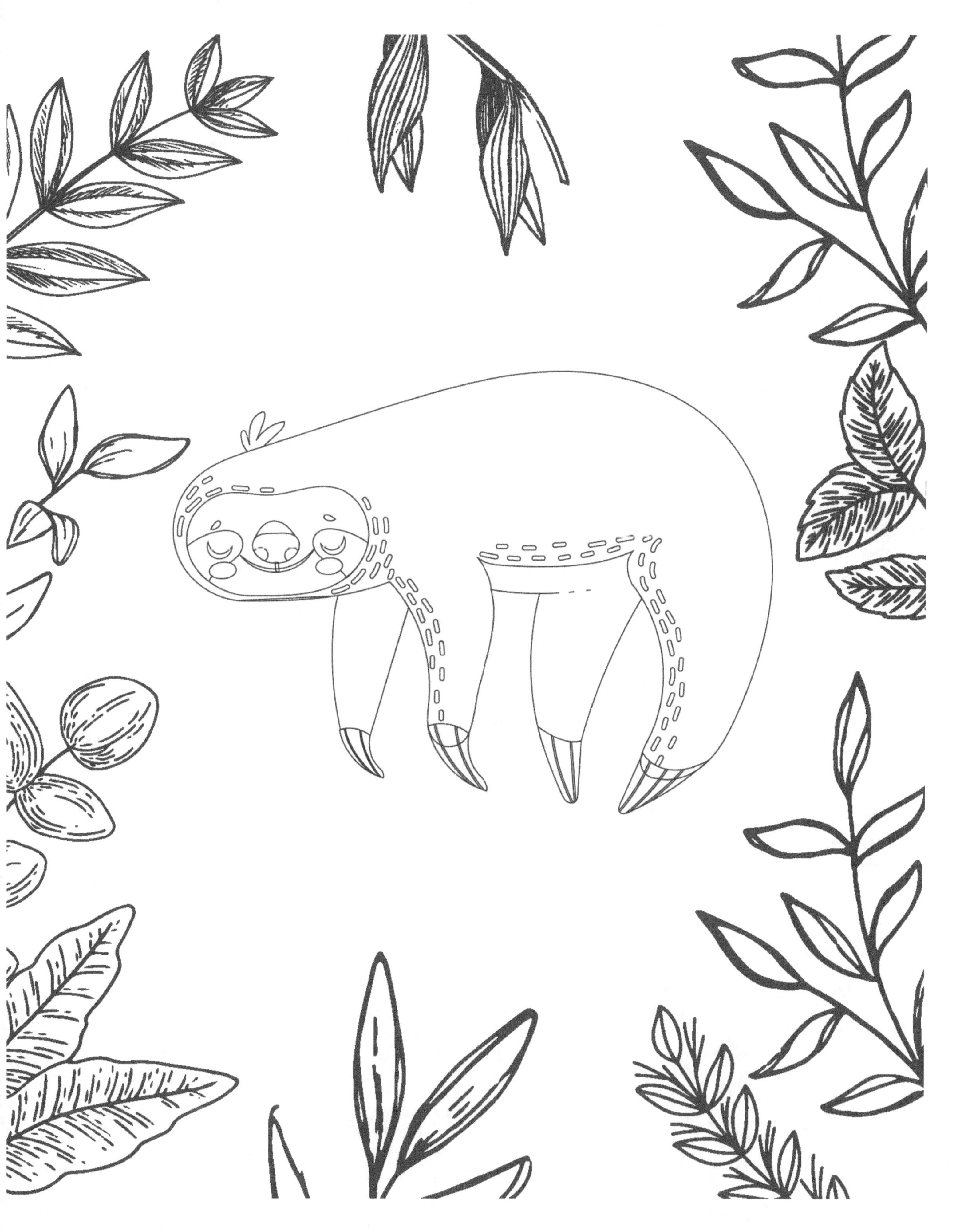

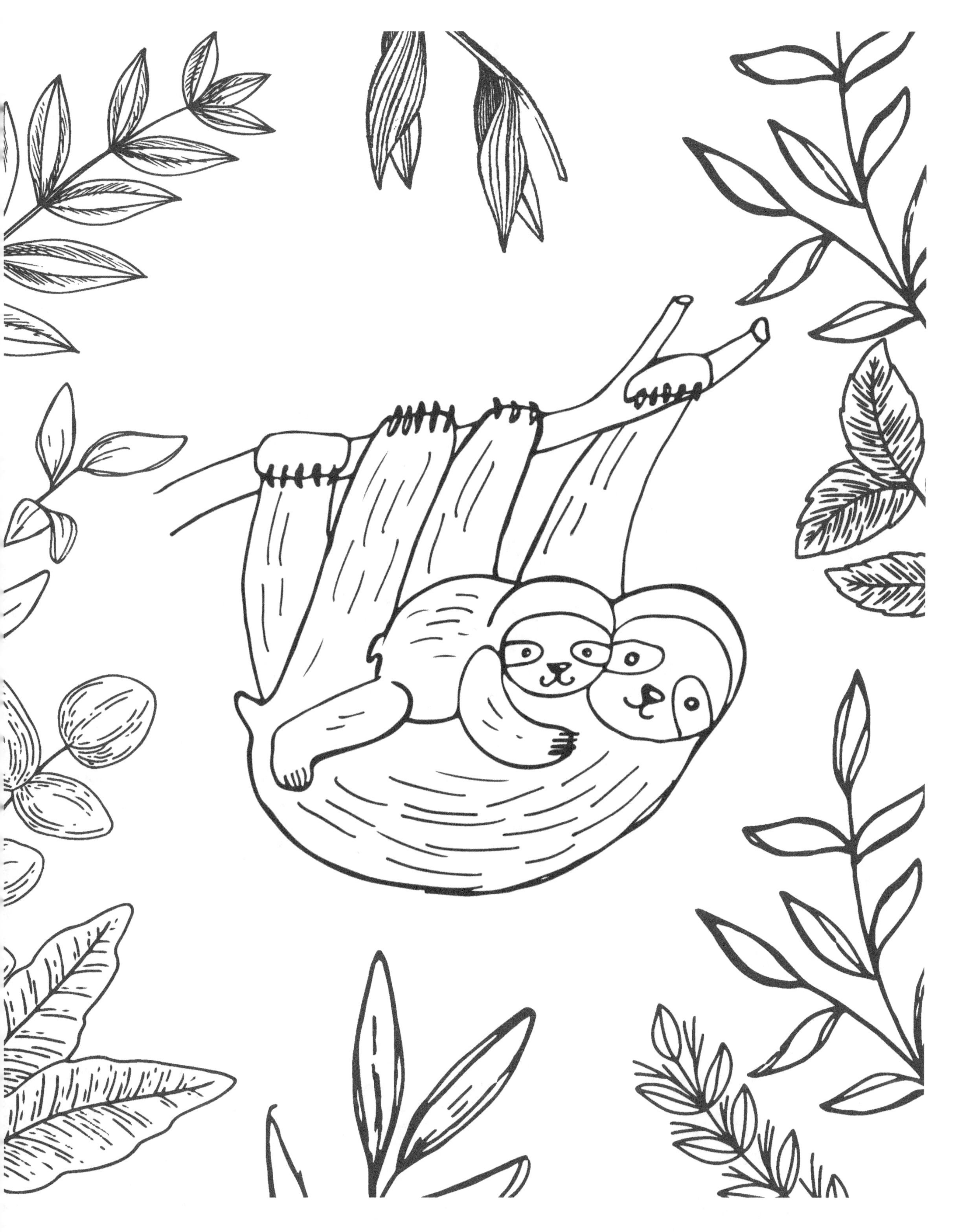

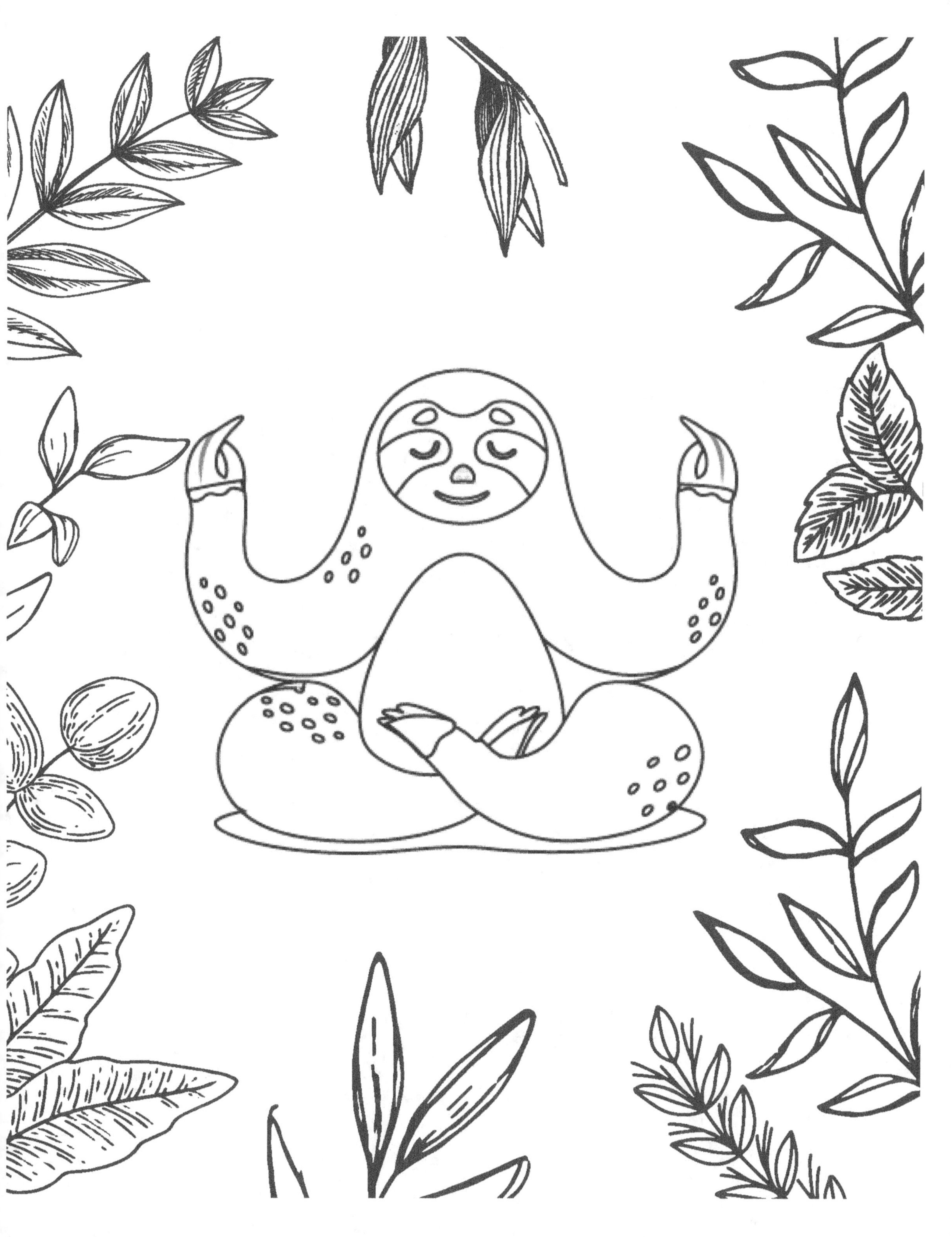

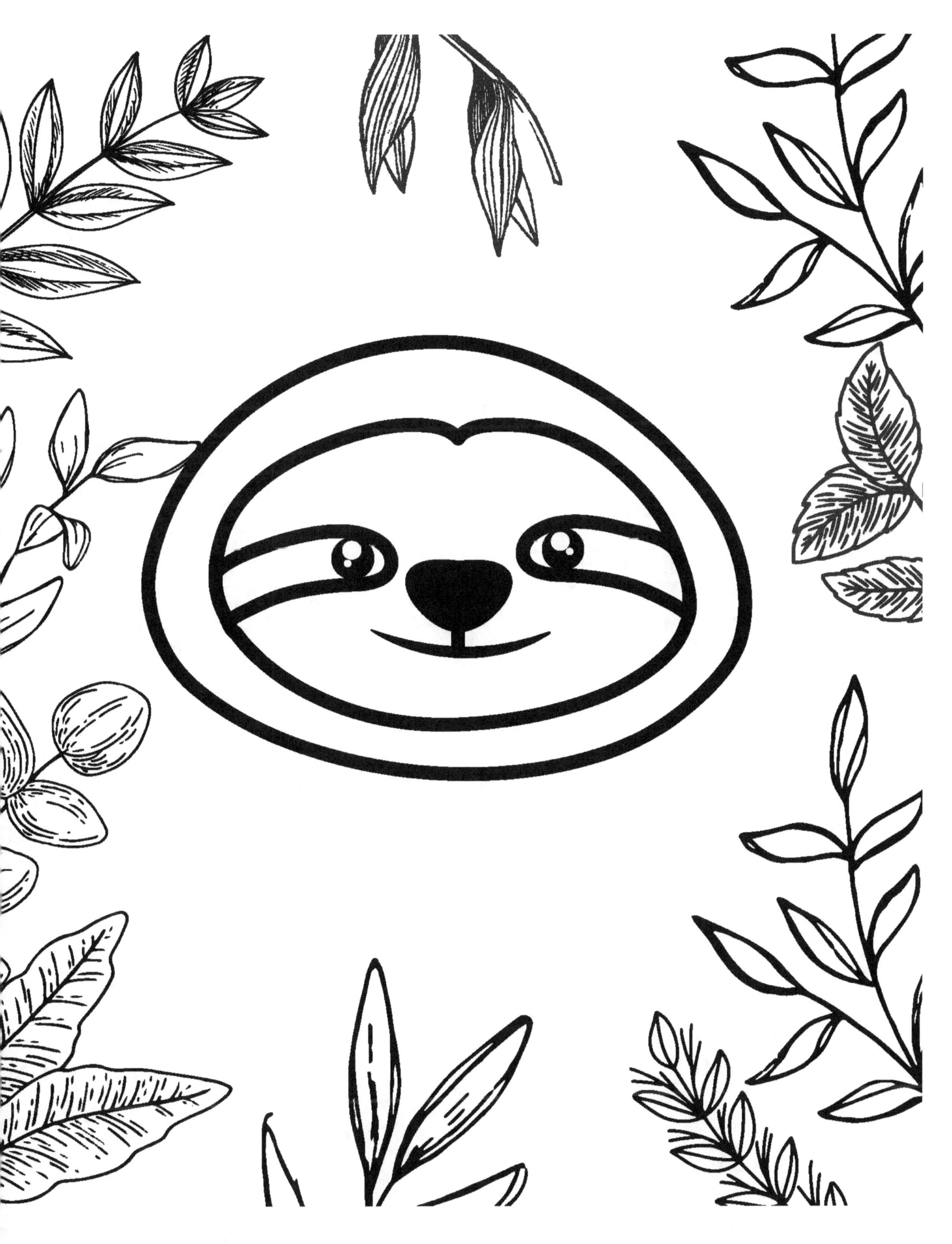

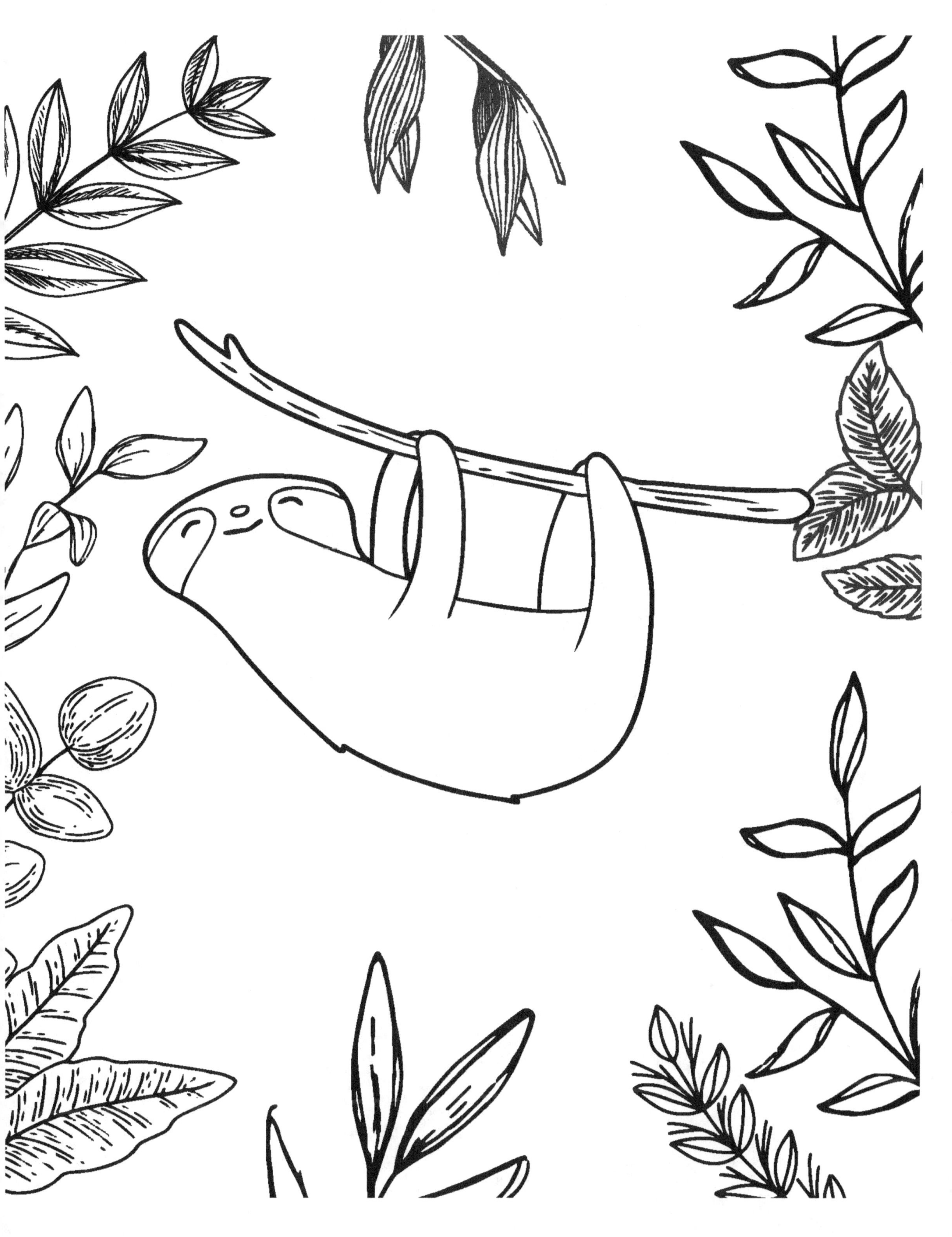

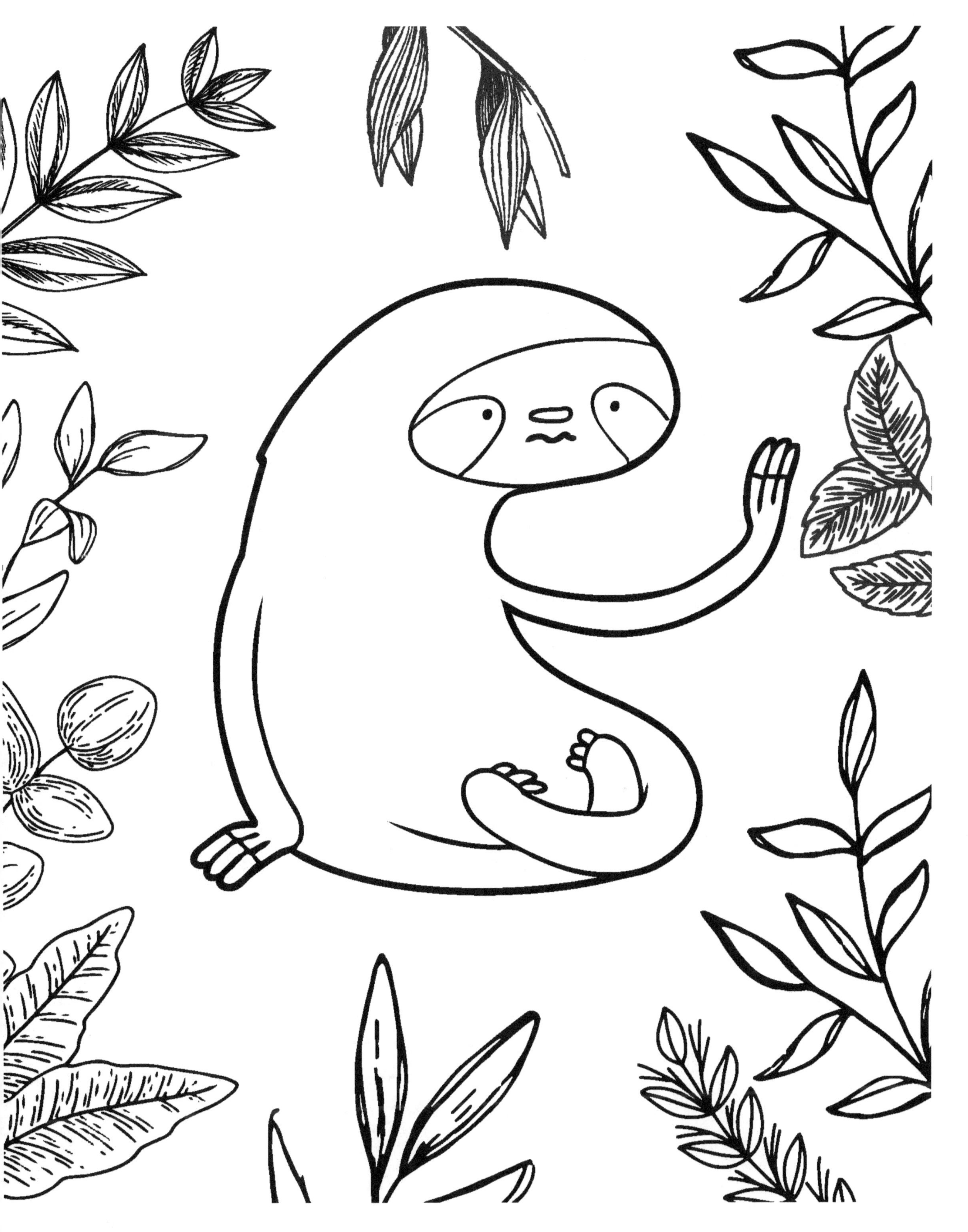

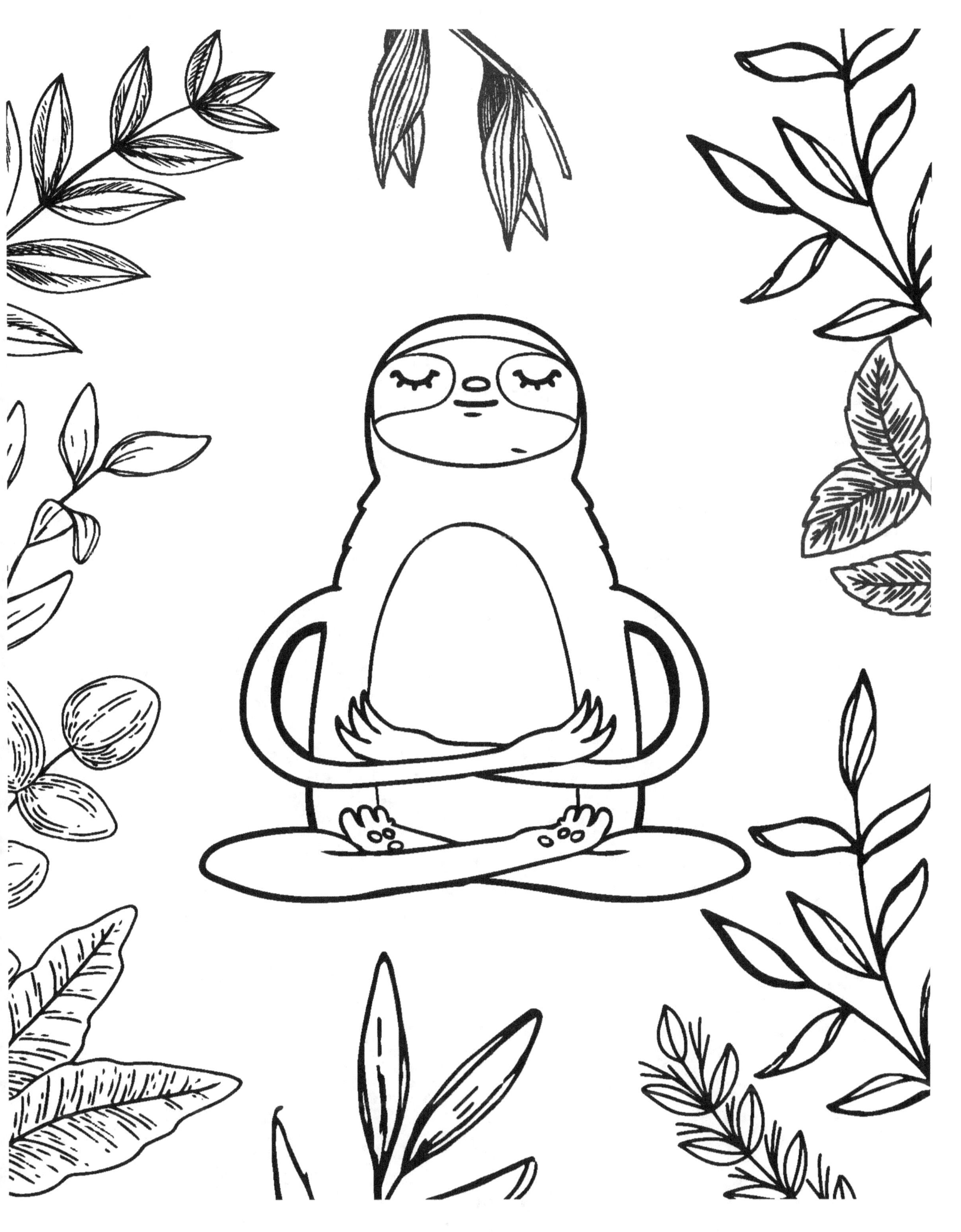

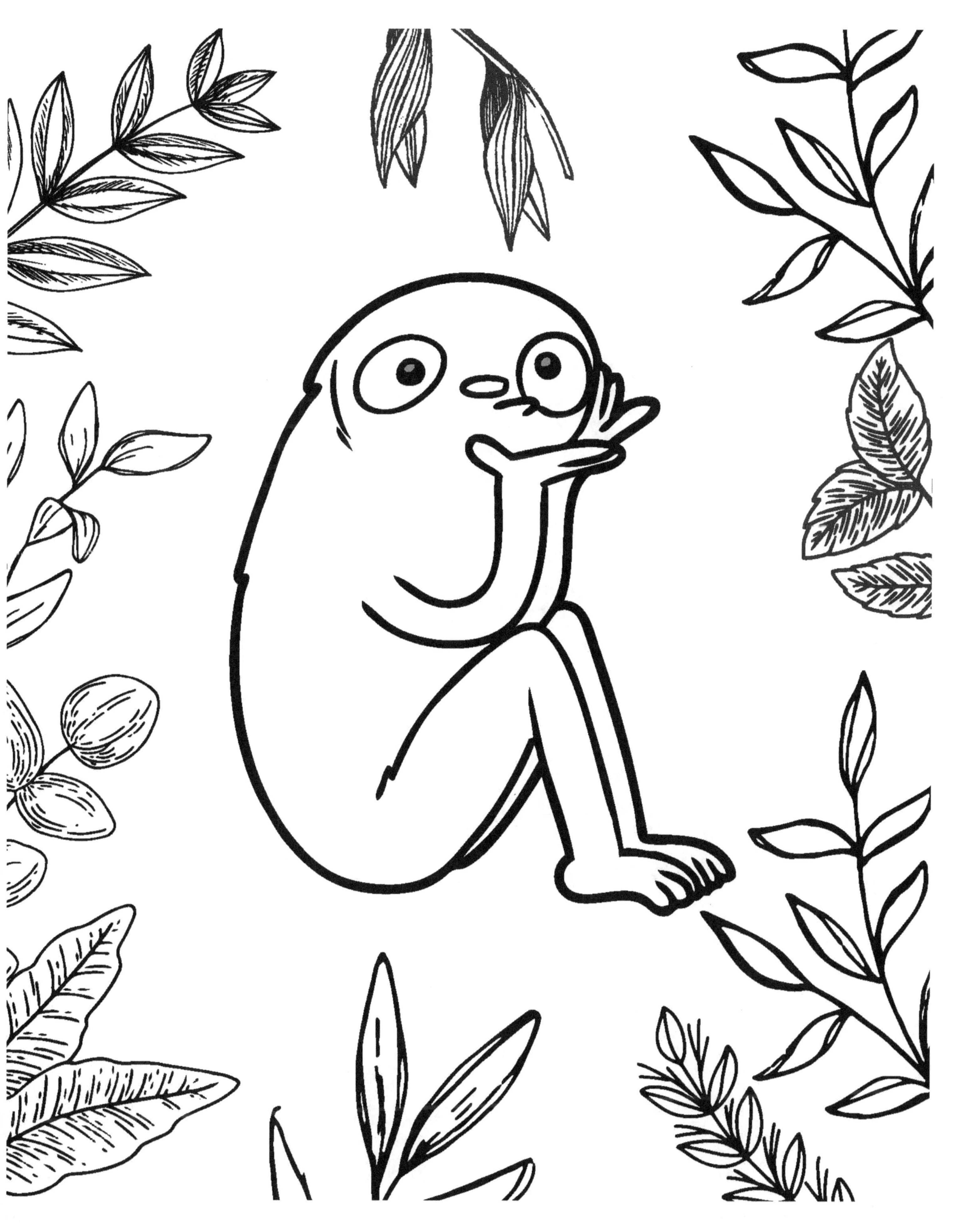

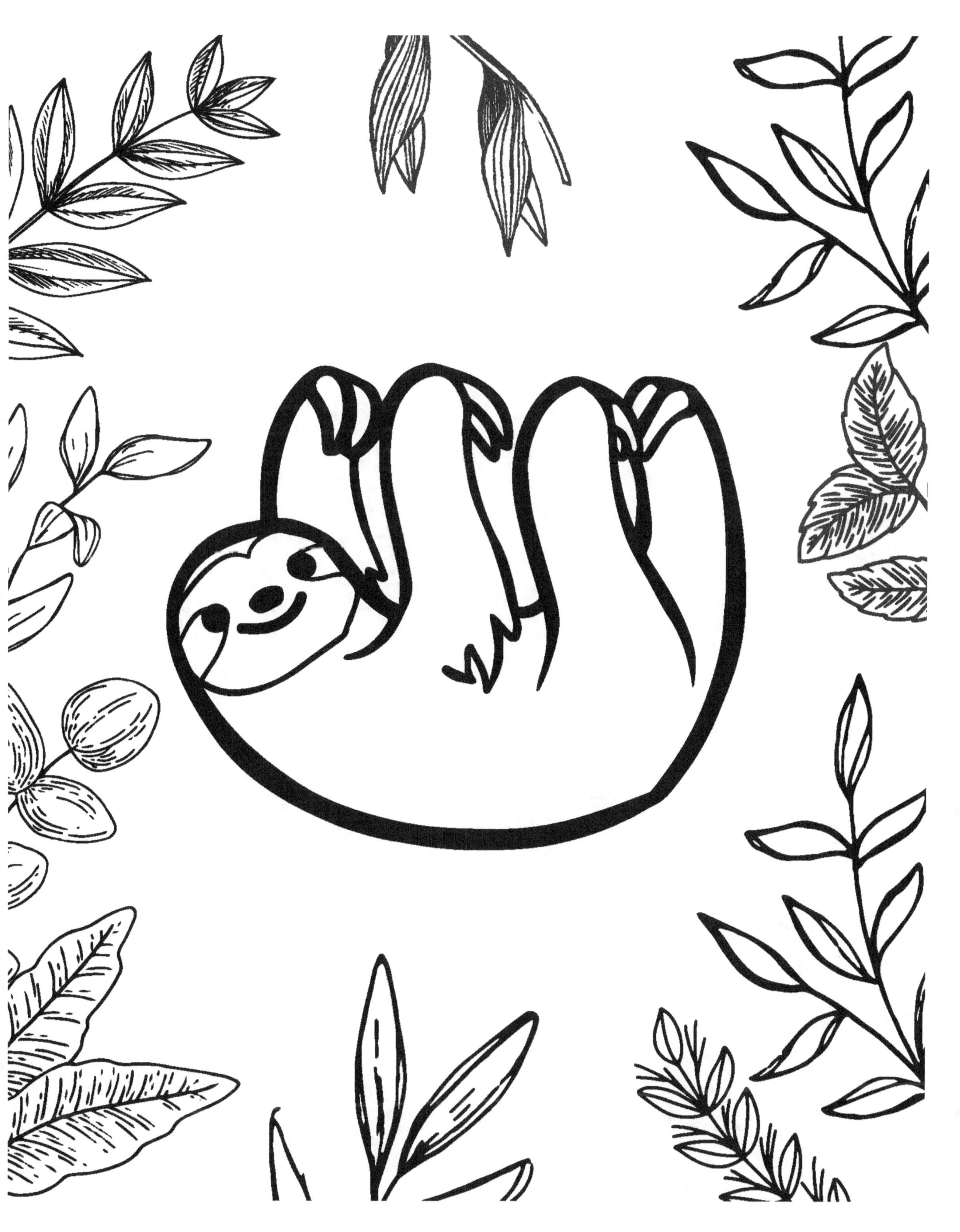

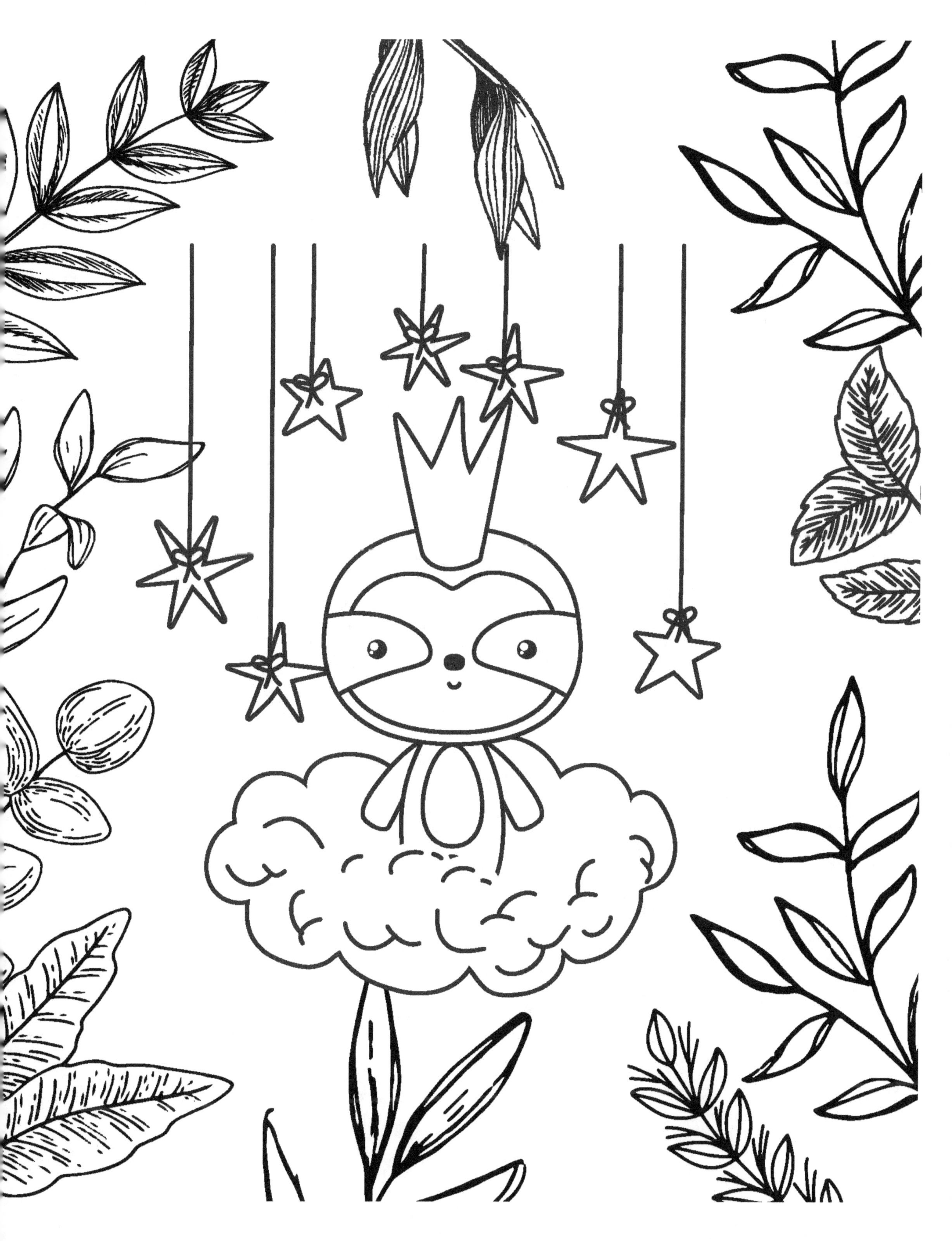

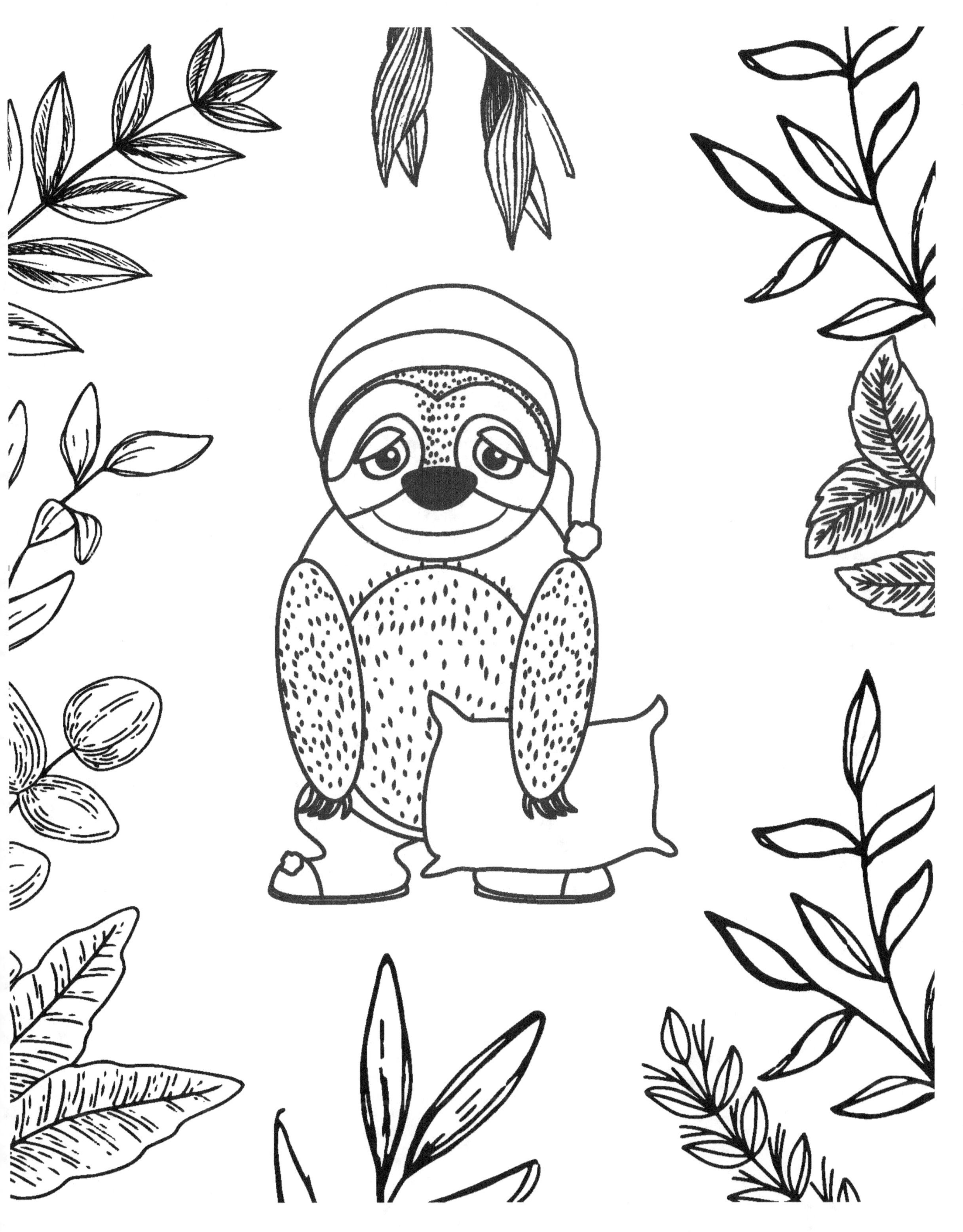

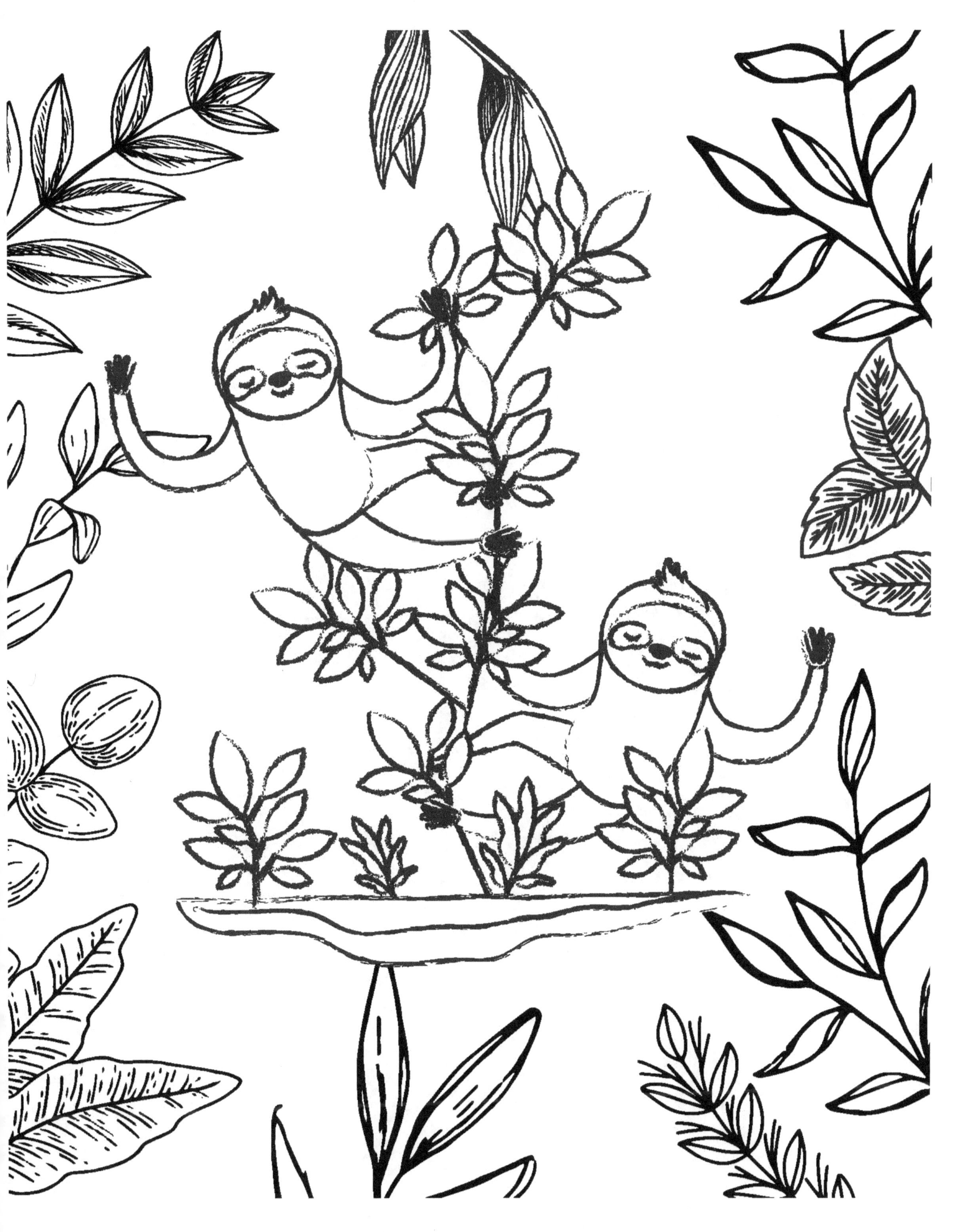

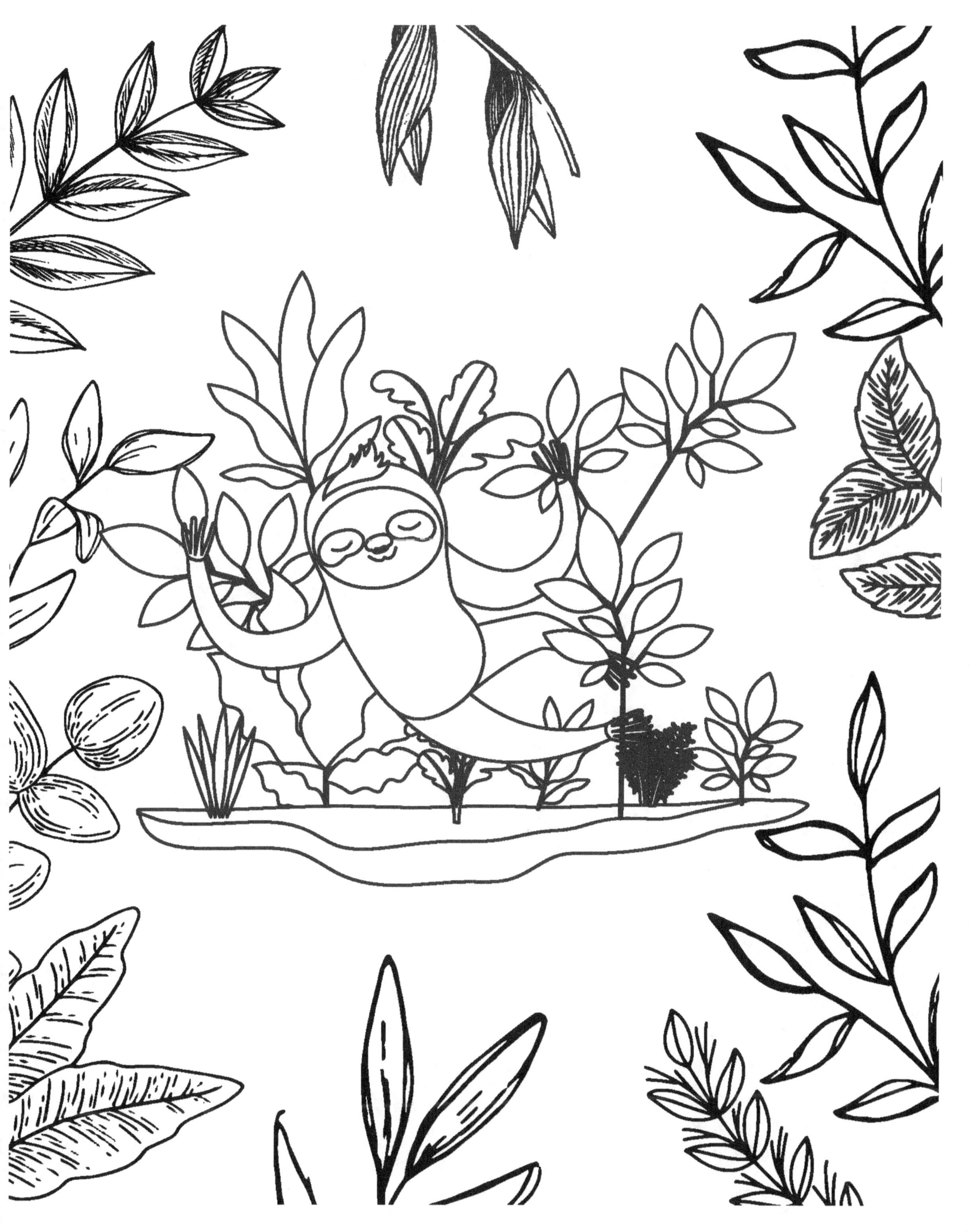

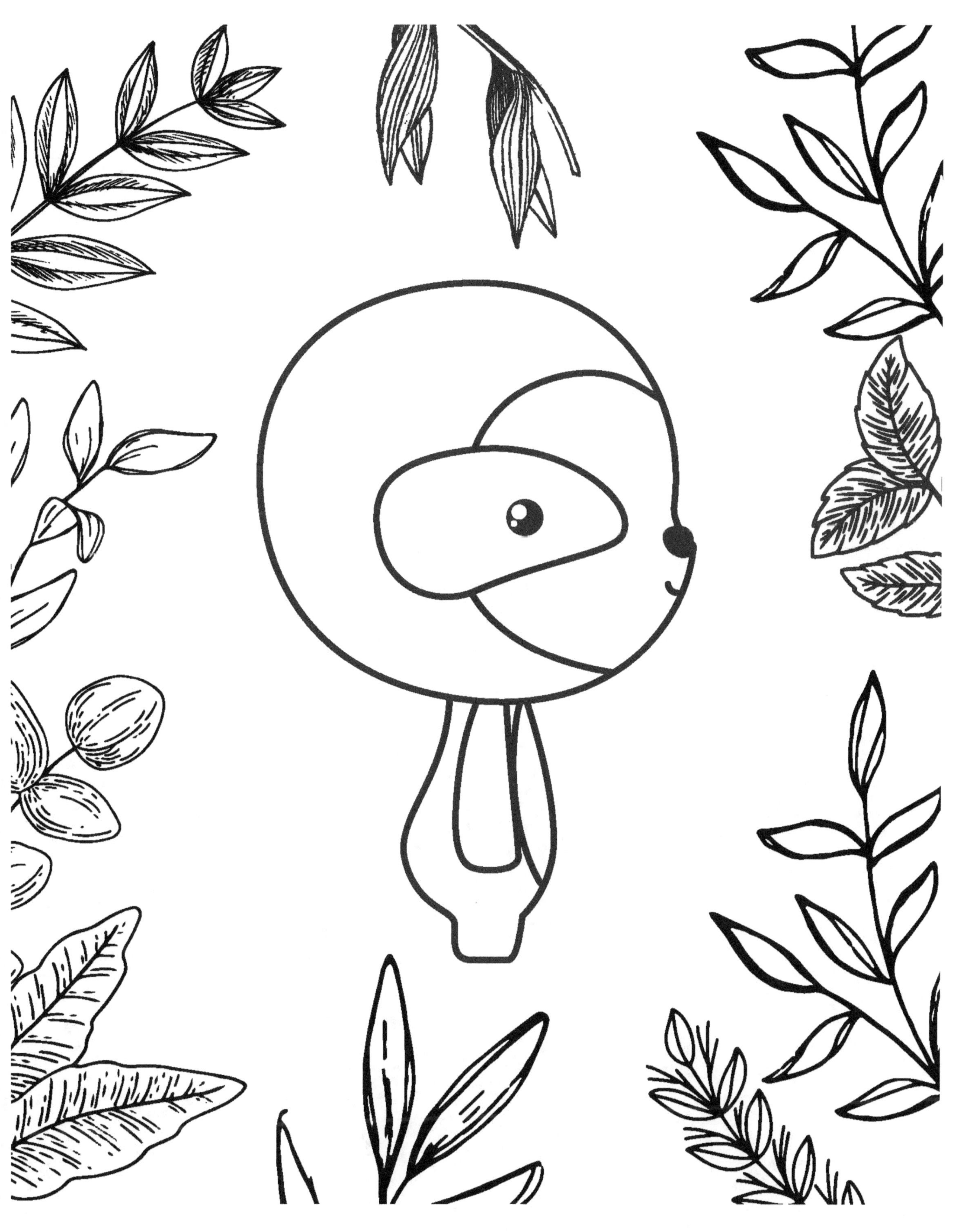

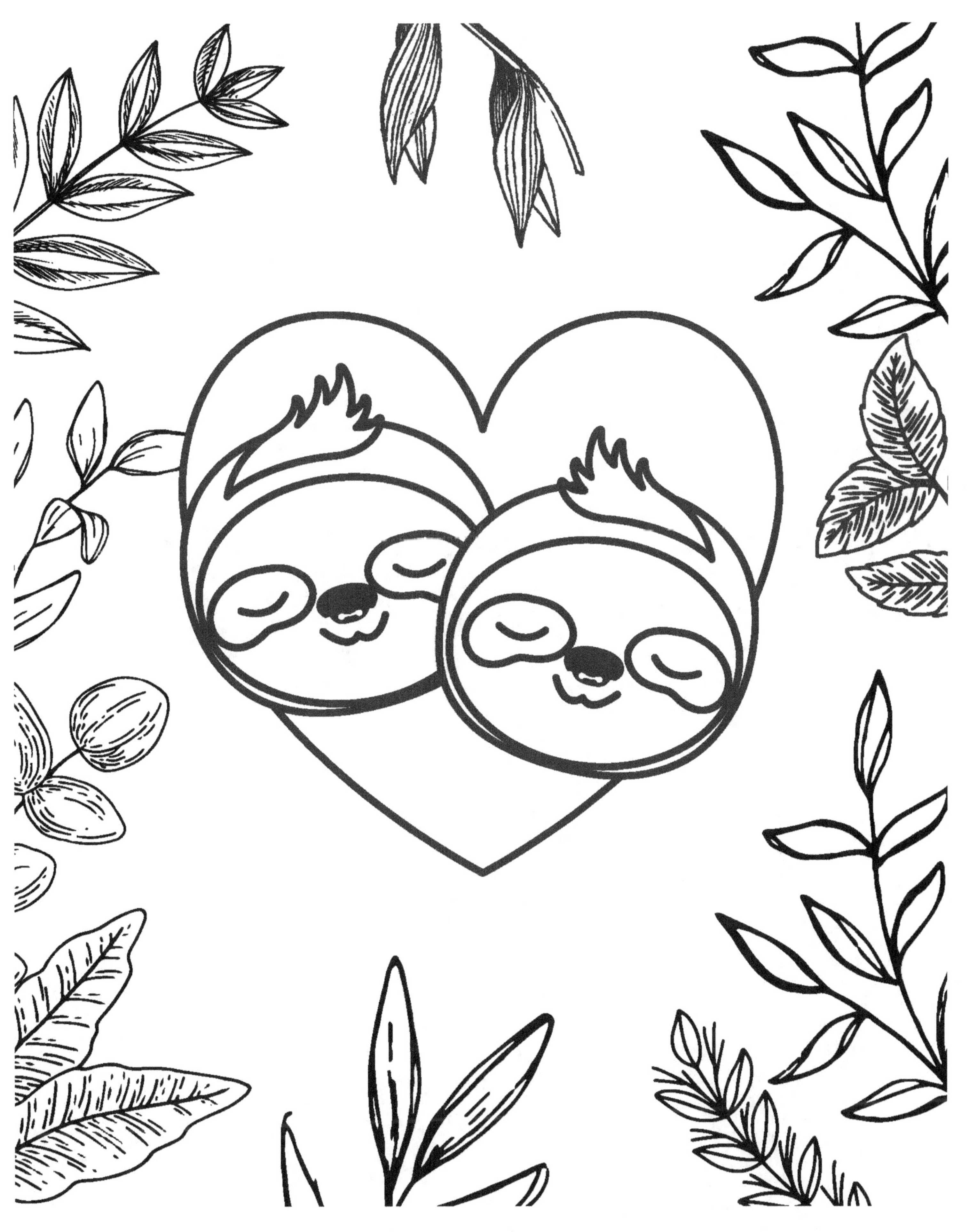

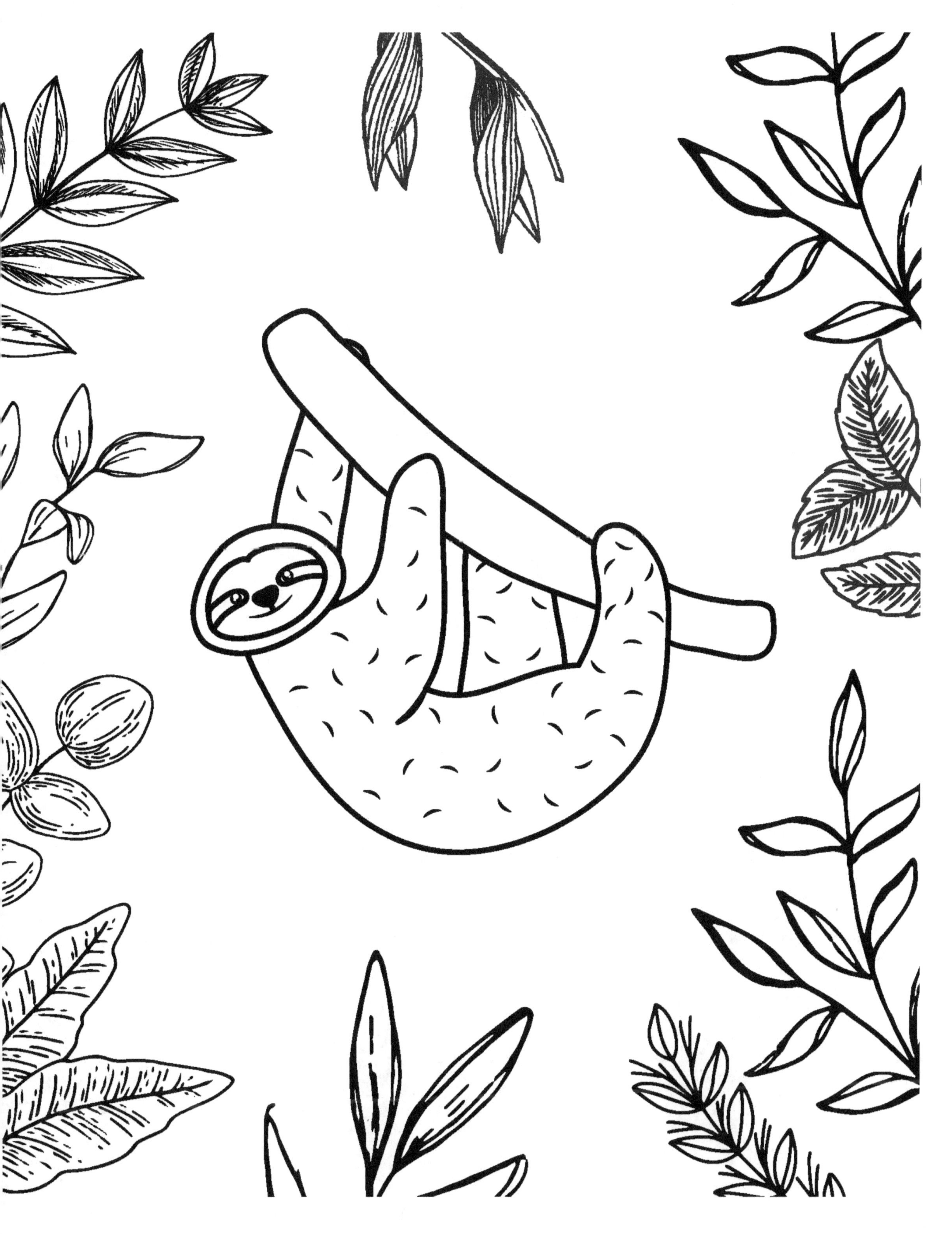

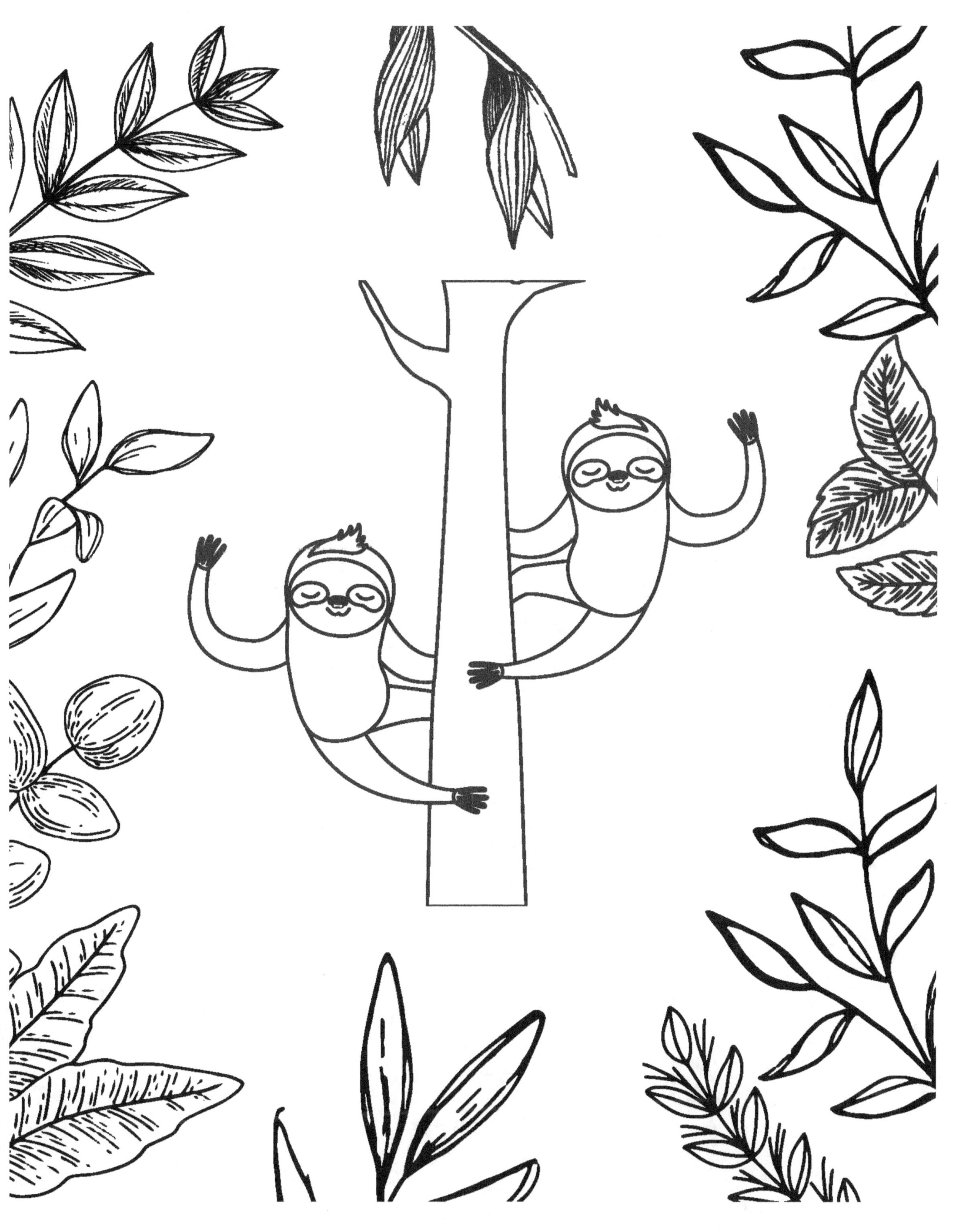

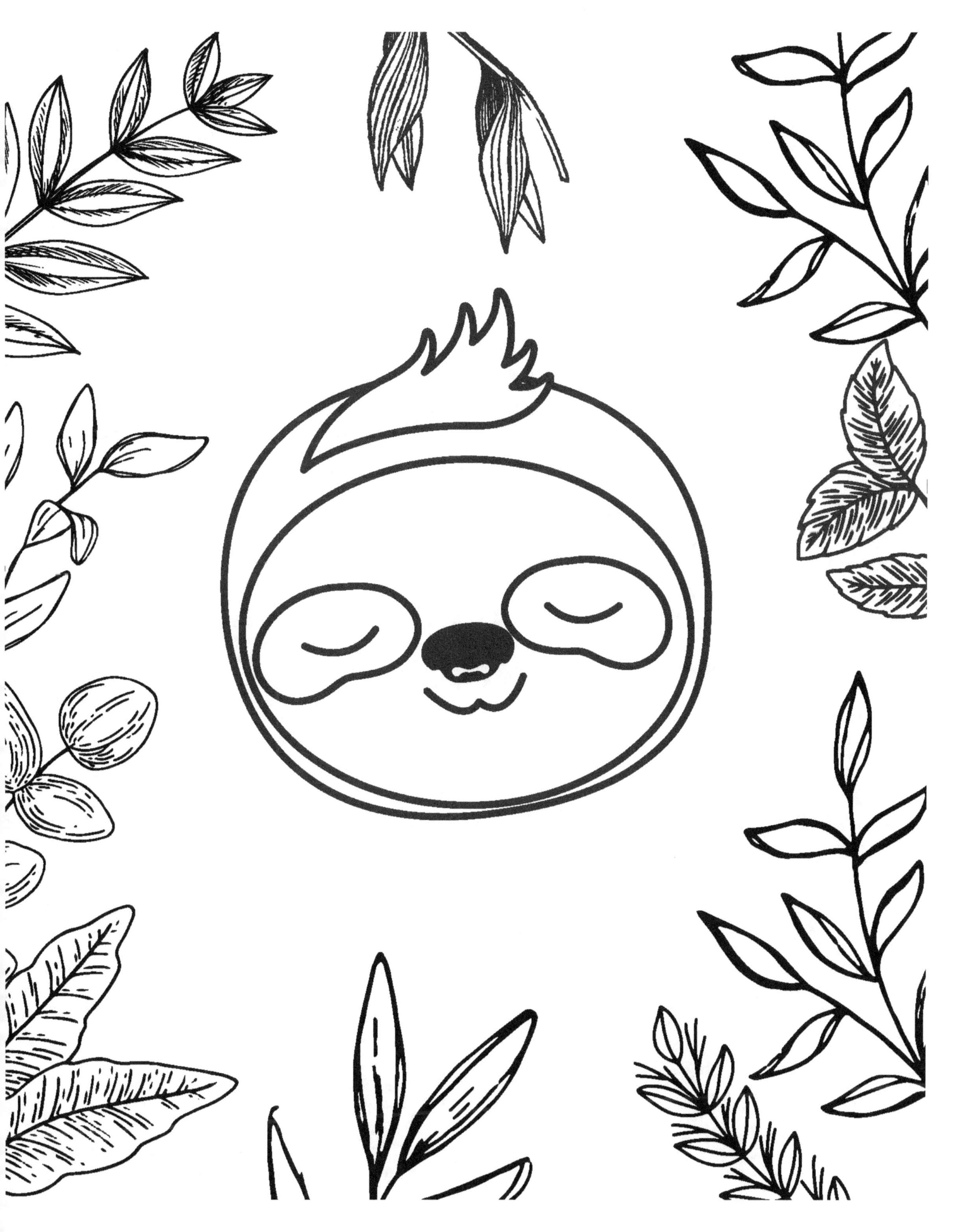

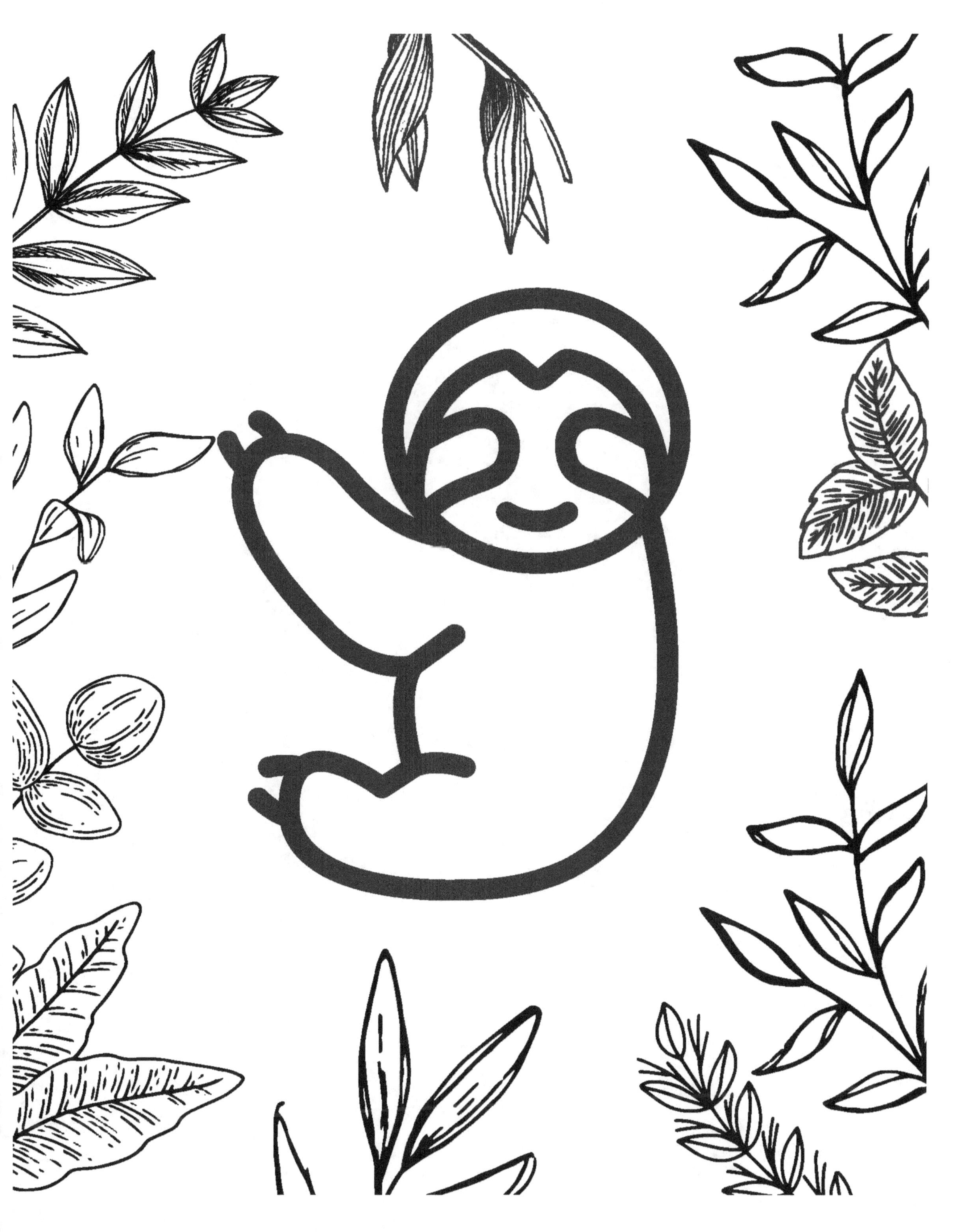

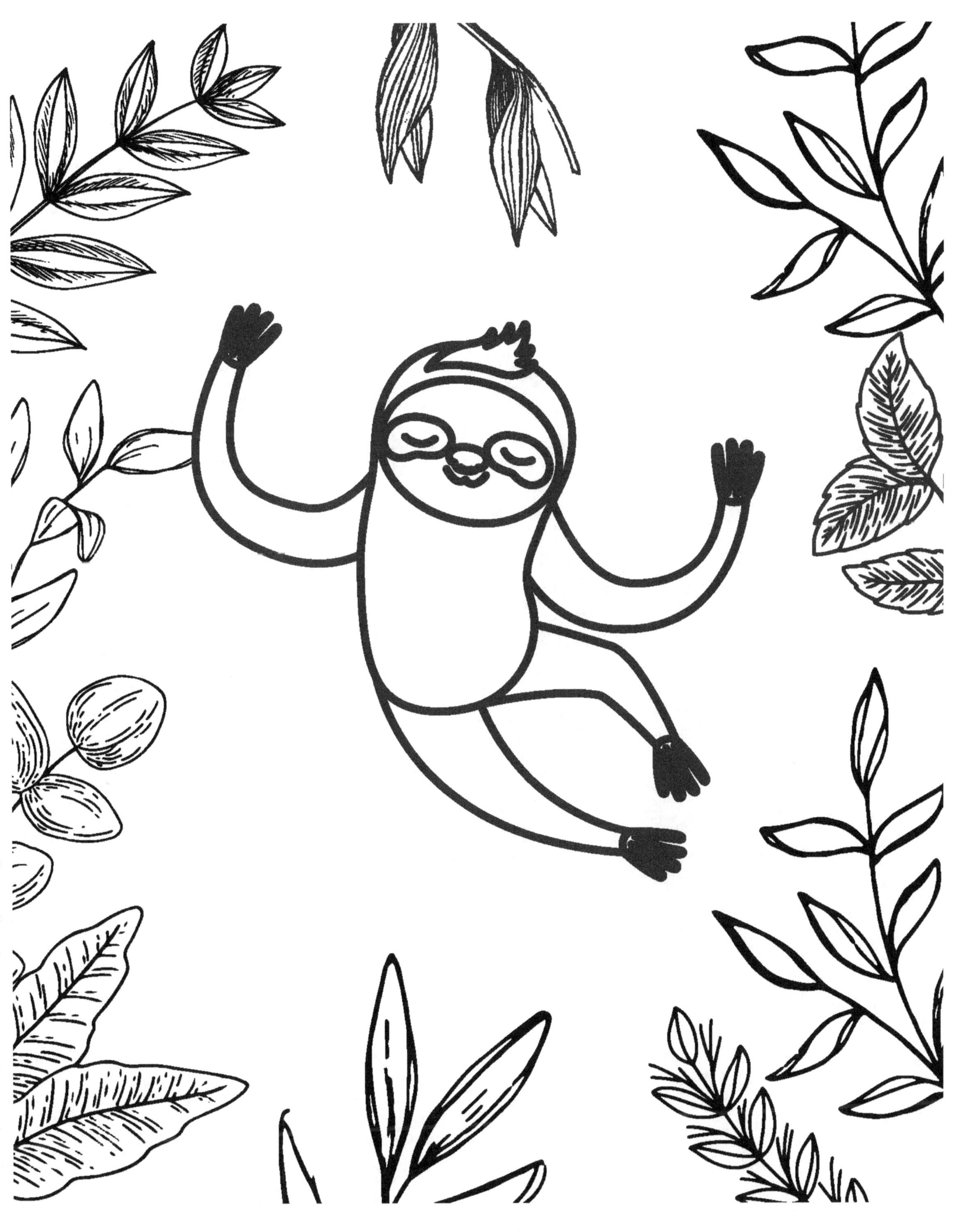

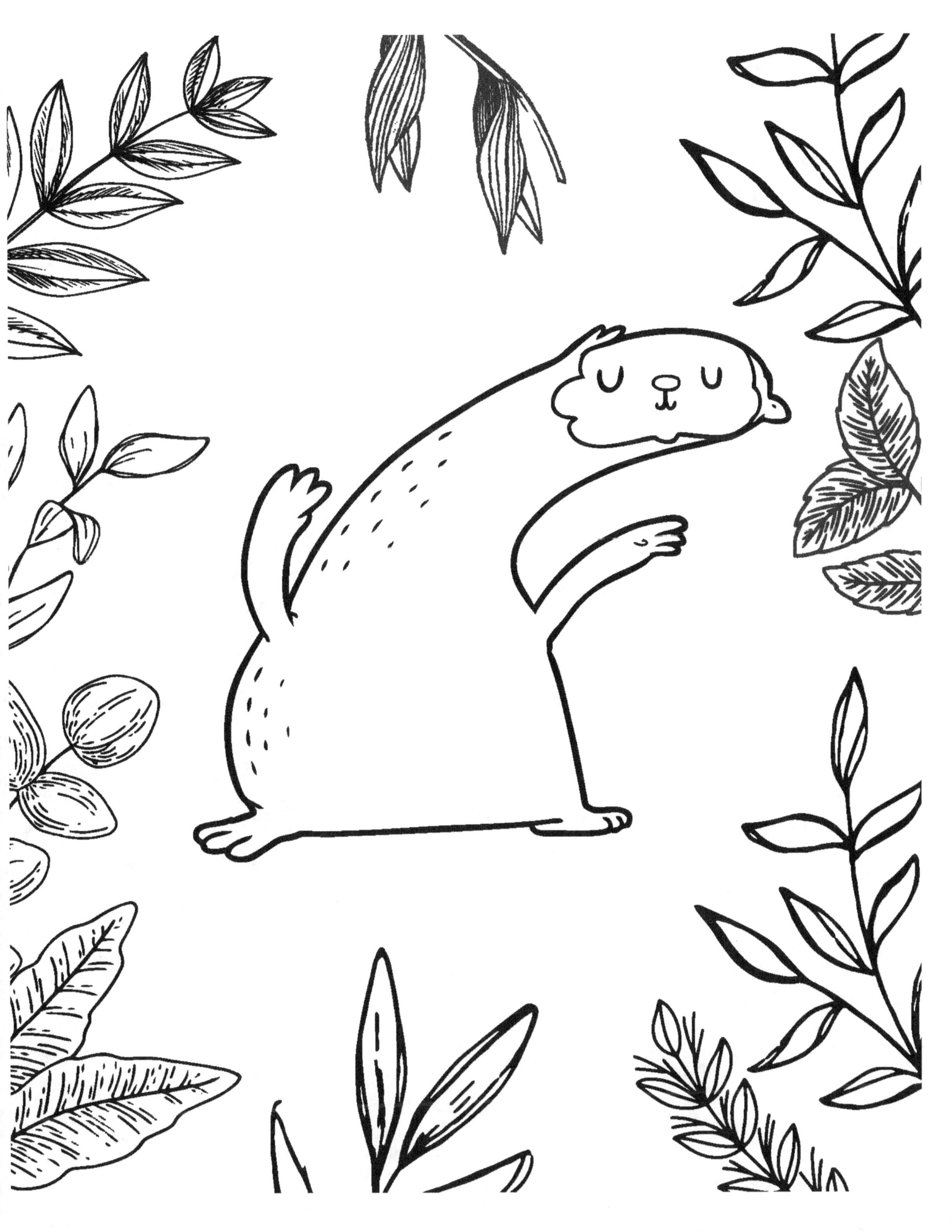

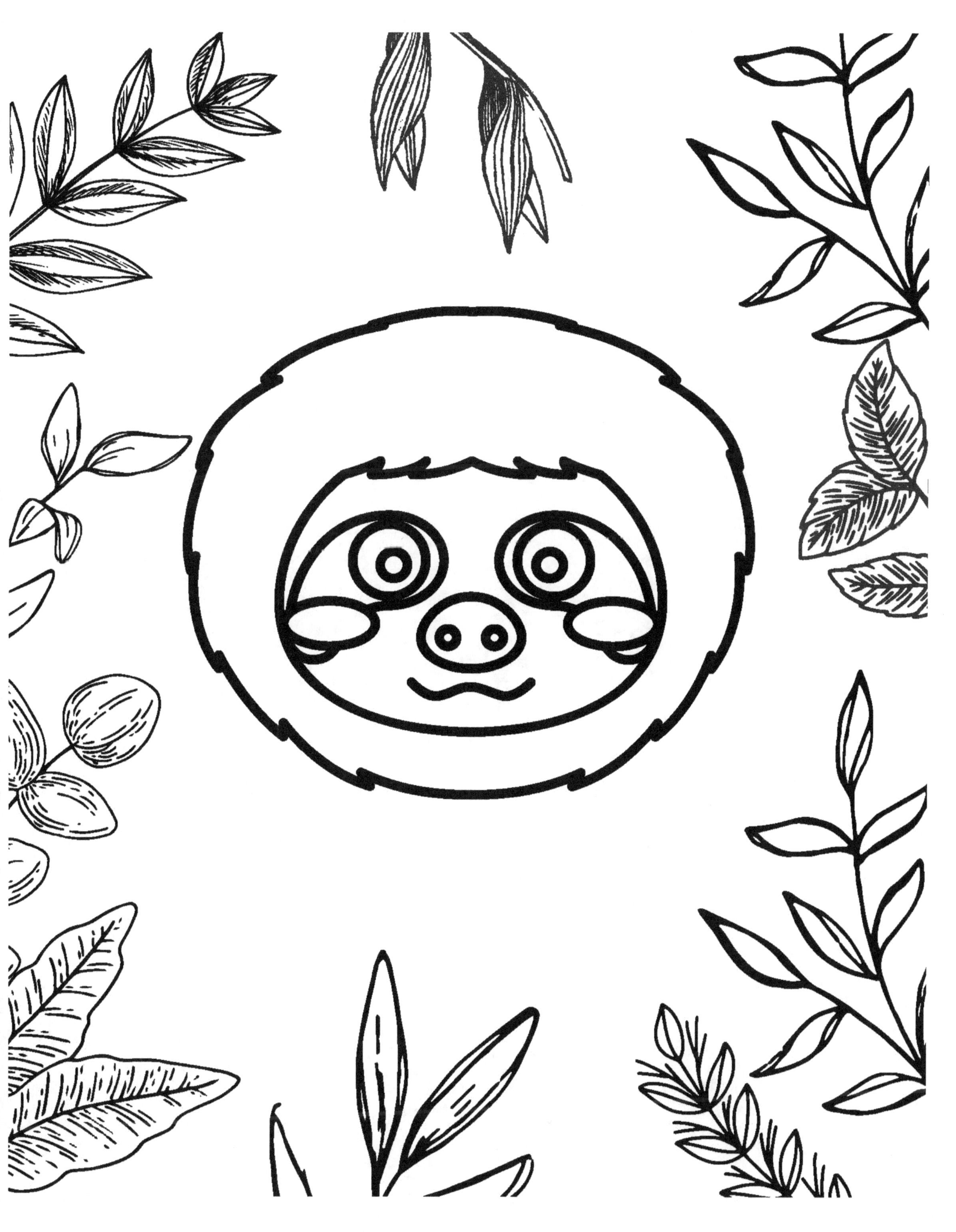

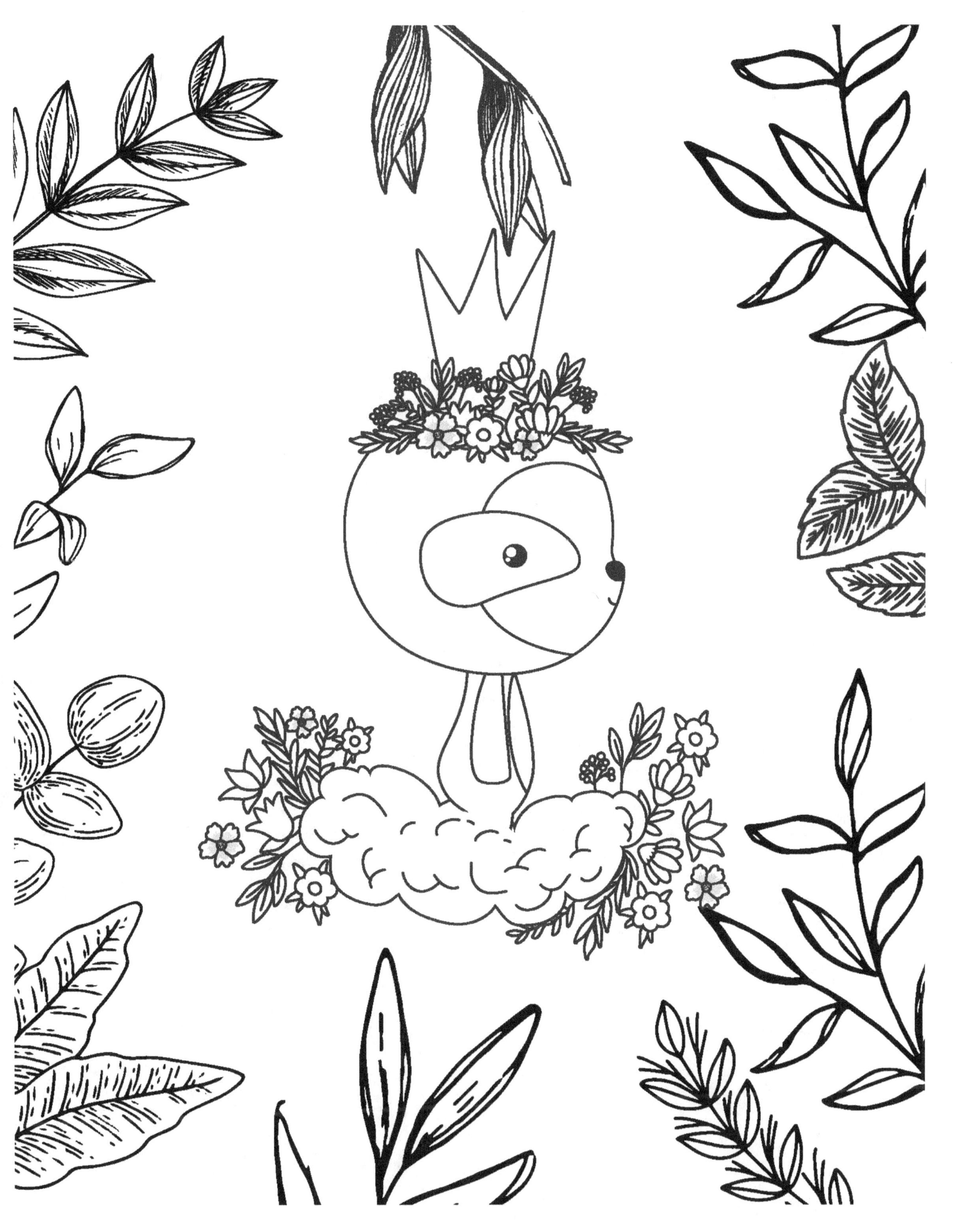

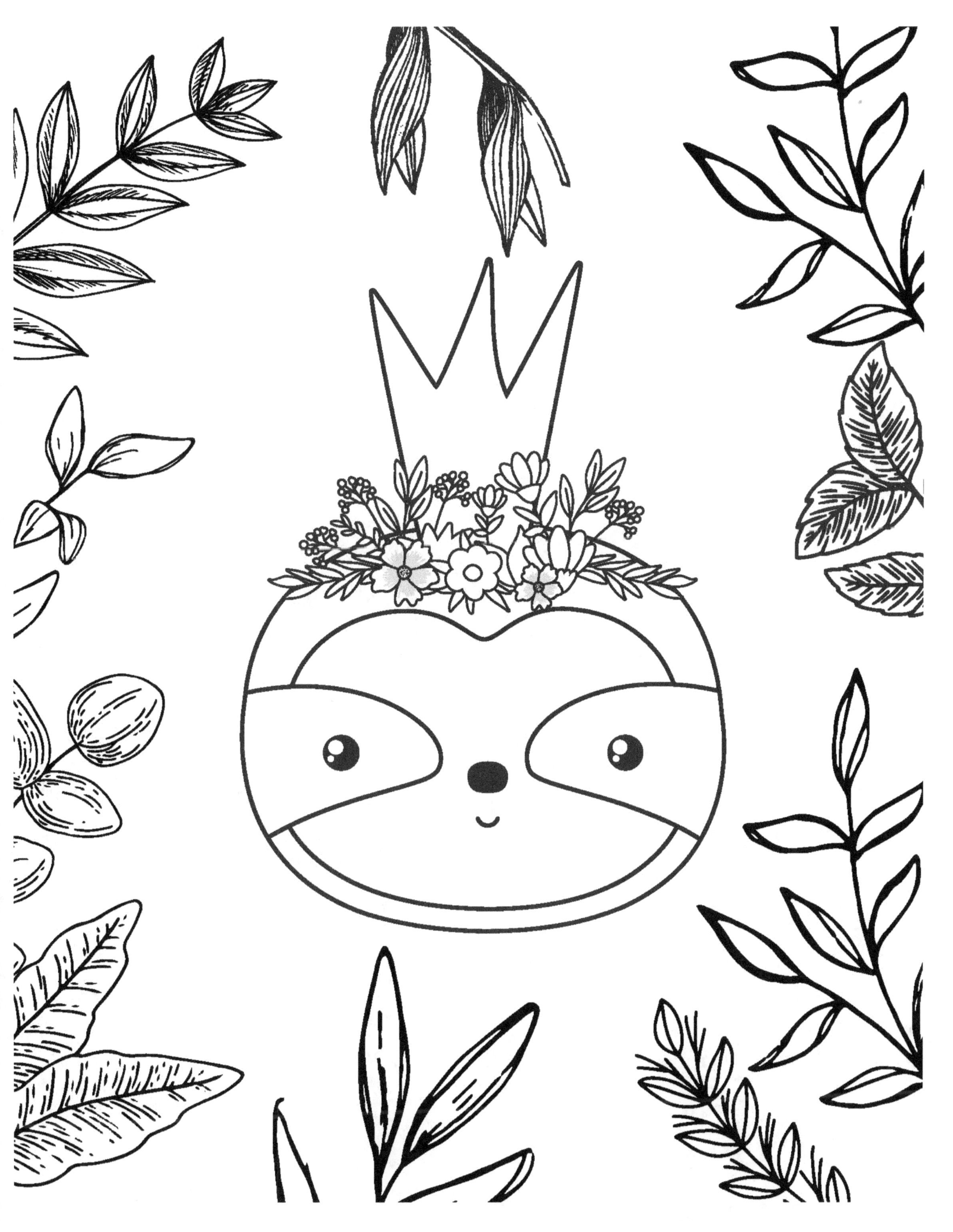

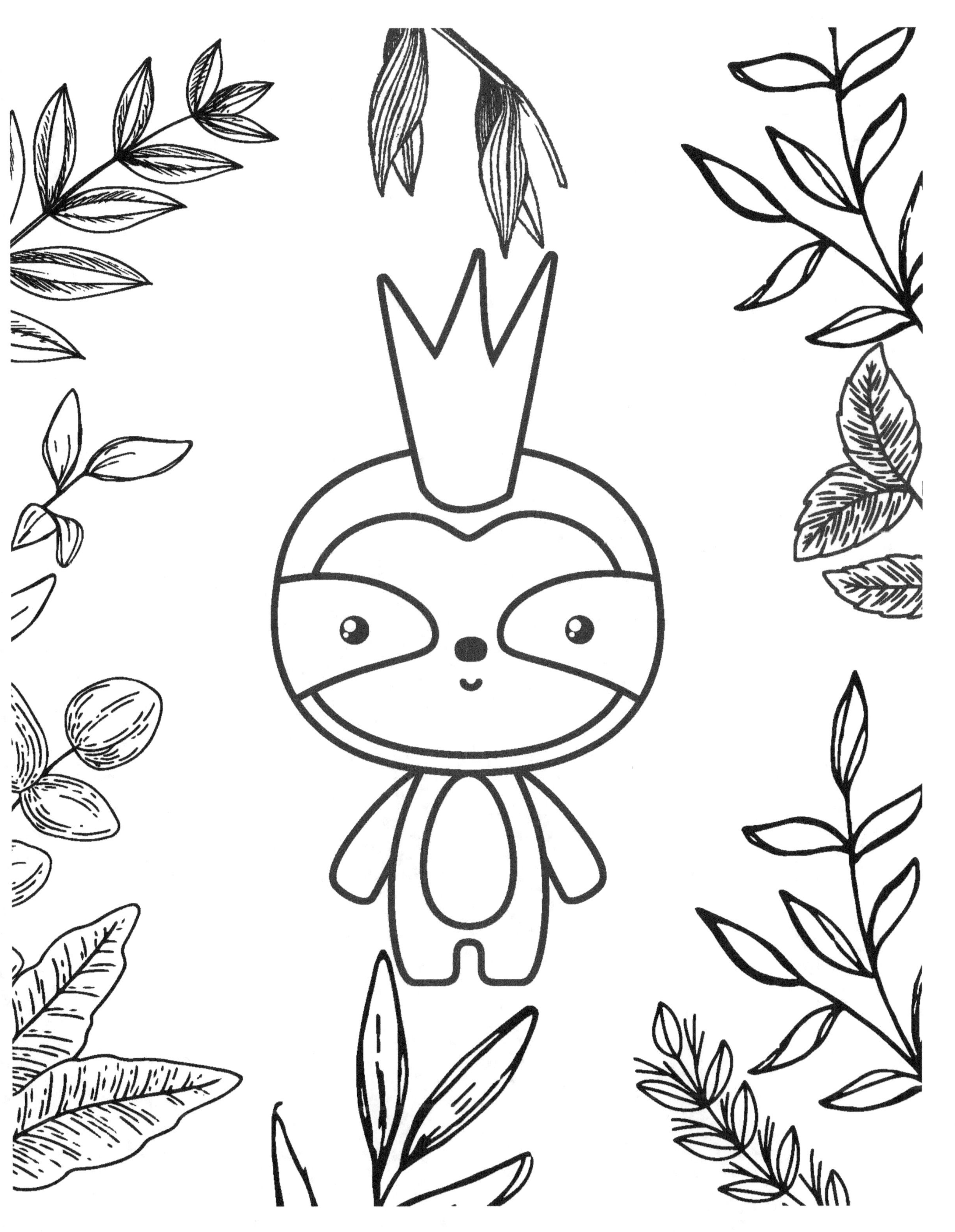

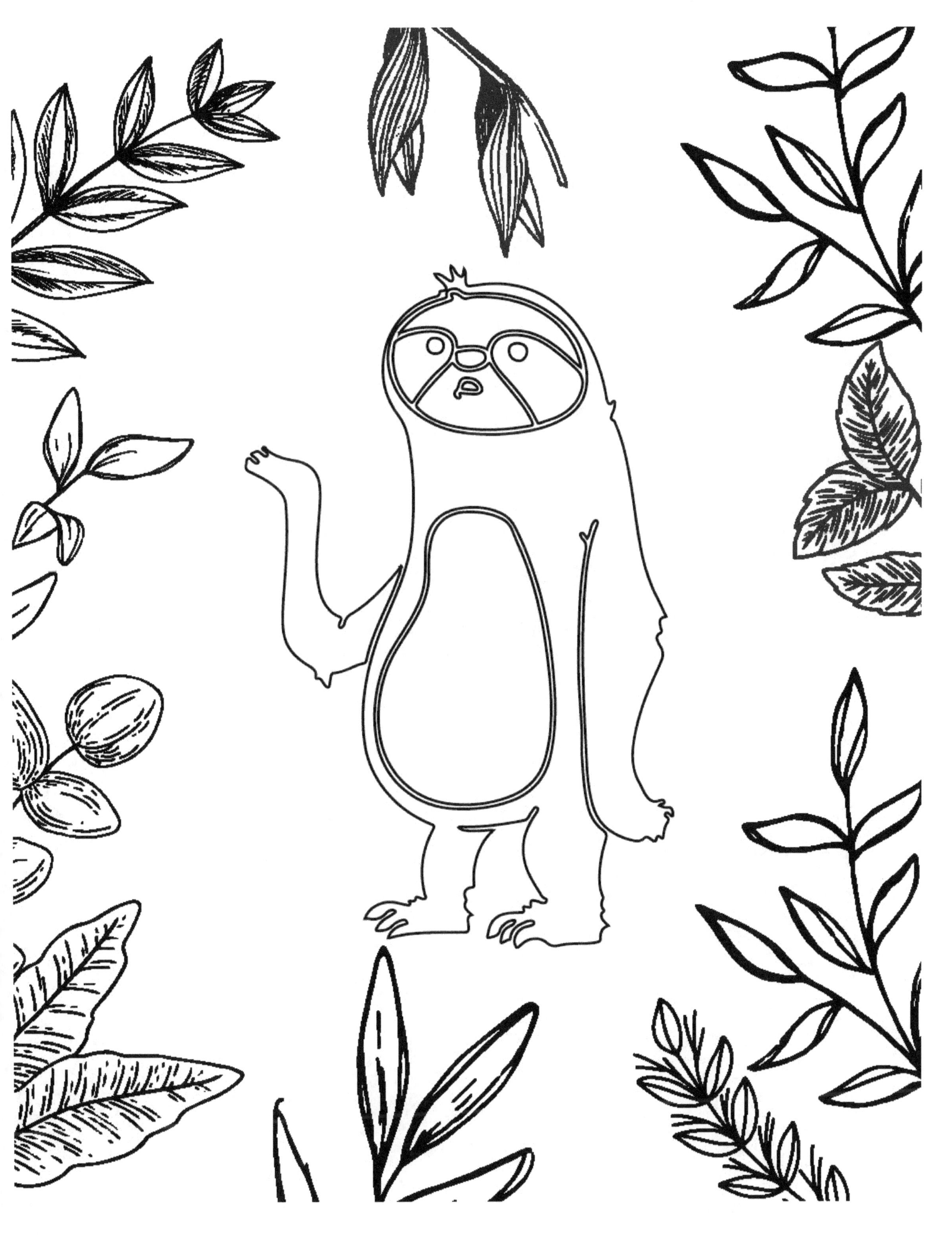

www.ingramcontent.com/pod-product-compliance
Lightning Source LLC
Chambersburg PA
CBHW081455250726
48662CB00009B/3097

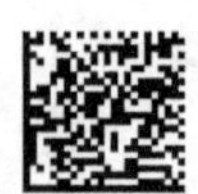
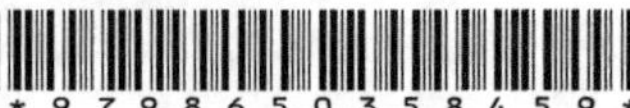